BASTIEN PIANO BASICS
SUPPLEMENTARY

A CELEBRATION OF NOTES

Naming, Drawing, Playing, Hearing

Book 1

BY JANE SMISOR BASTIEN

KJOS NEIL A. KJOS MUSIC COMPANY • SAN DIEGO, CALIFORNIA

Preface

A **Celebration of Notes, Book 1** contains exercises for naming, drawing, playing, and hearing *all* of the notes on the staff. It is very important for students to understand the relationships (by skips and steps) between all of these notes and their exact location on the keyboard. We feel that much emphasis should be placed on learning to recognize all of the staff notes quickly. This book should help your students achieve this goal.

Neil A. Kjos Music Company
James Bastien
Jane Smisor Bastien

About the Composer

Jane Smisor Bastien teaches pre-schoolers through advanced high school students in her La Jolla, California, studio. She is very active in the San Diego music teacher organizations.

All of her music is written to fulfill her students' needs. Her busy five-day-a-week teaching schedule is both inspiration and proving ground for her teaching concepts and musical compositions.

For many years, Mrs. Bastien was director of the Preparatory Department at Tulane University in New Orleans. It was for her students there that she first started writing. Since then she and her husband, James, have produced music and methods for all ages.

Jane Smisor Bastien received a Bachelor of Arts, Phi Beta Kappa, from Barnard College in New York City and a Master of Arts from Columbia University, Teachers College.

Mrs. Bastien has presented numerous seminars and workshops throughout the United States and in many foreign countries where the Bastien books have been translated. The Bastiens are the parents of two adult daughters.

To the Teacher

A Celebration of Notes, Book 1 contains 11 pages of ear training activities for your students along with the written note exercises. We suggest playing each example a minimum of three times, so the student will feel secure. In addition, we recommend using only steps and skips (2nds and 3rds) for the student to hear and write.

This book may be introduced when a student reaches page 52 of *Bastien Piano Basics, Piano, Primer Level (WP200)*, and used simultaneously with *Piano, Level 1 (WP201)*. We also recommend using the *Bastien Music Flashcards (GP27)* to help students recognize and play notes. There are specific exercises on pages 28, 30, and 31 to help the student recognize all of the notes on the staff in one minute and thus become a member of the "One-Minute Club." Rewards for students who are members of the "One-Minute Club" are provided in *Bastien Student Boosters (WP225)*.

ISBN 0-8497-9410-2

Skips, Steps, Repeats

Notes may move three different ways: skips, steps, repeats.

Skip	Step	Repeat
skips a letter skips a finger	next letter next finger	same letter same finger

1. Write "sk" for skip; "st" for step, and "r" for repeat.

2. Circle skips and steps that move **up** with red.   Circle skips and steps that move **down** with blue.
   Circle **repeats** with green.

3. Listen and write whether your teacher plays a skip, step, or repeat. Listen again and tell whether it
   moves up or down.

daddy

1. _____   3. _____   5. _____   7. _____

2. _____   4. _____   6. _____   8. _____

4. Draw the following skips, steps, and repeats.

step up   skip down   repeat   skip up   step down

repeat   skip up   step down   skip down   step up   repeat

5. Listen and draw the note your teacher plays after the given note. Is it a skip, step, or repeat? Does it move up or down?

1.   2.   3.   4.   5.

6.   7.   8.   9.   10.

6. Draw the following skips, steps, and repeats.

line note repeat   skip up   step down   step up   skip down   space note repeat

Line Notes on the Staff

G is on the bottom line of the bass clef.
From a line to a line is a skip.
A skip up from G is B etc.

7. Draw the letter names of the notes on the lines of the staff.
Play these notes in the correct place on the keyboard.

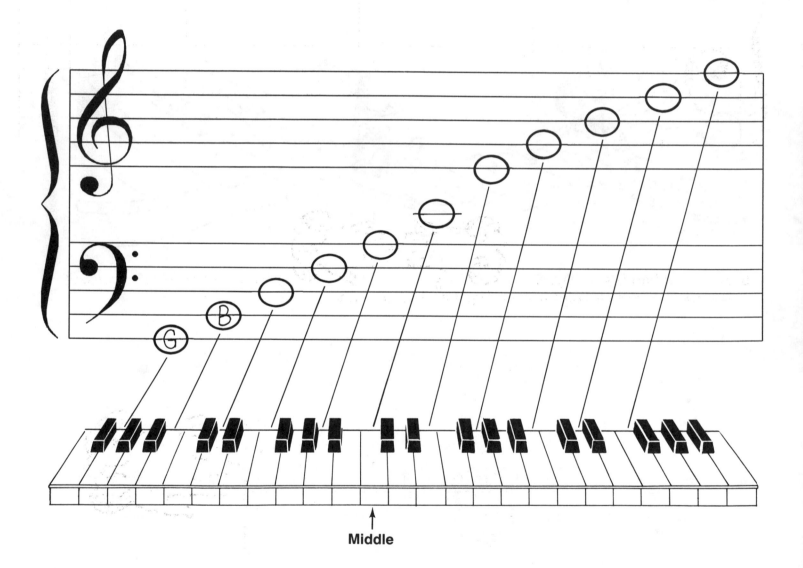

Middle

Notes on the lower part of the keyboard are written on the lower part of the staff.
Notes in the middle of the keyboard are written on the middle part of the staff.
Notes on the upper part of the keyboard are written on the upper part of the staff.

Practice naming and playing the line notes on the *Bastien Music Flashcards* until you can recognize them easily.

8. Write the letter names of the line notes 4 times a day. Say the letters aloud as you write them. Memorize these letters. Continue, on blank music paper, to write and say the line notes 4 times every day.

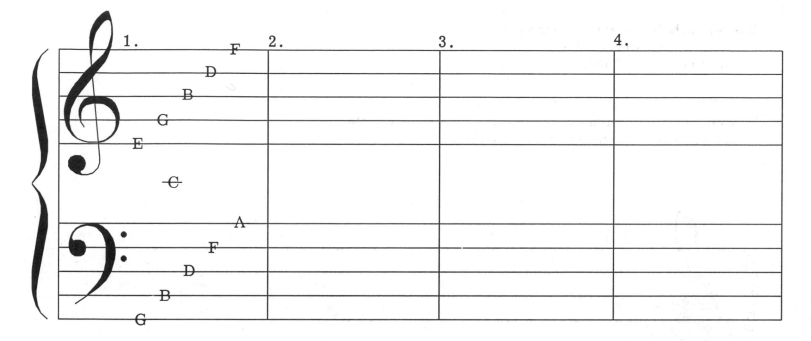

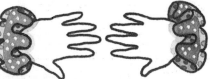

9. Turn your hands sideways (LH RH). Let your fingers represent the lines of the staff. Point to each finger and say its name.

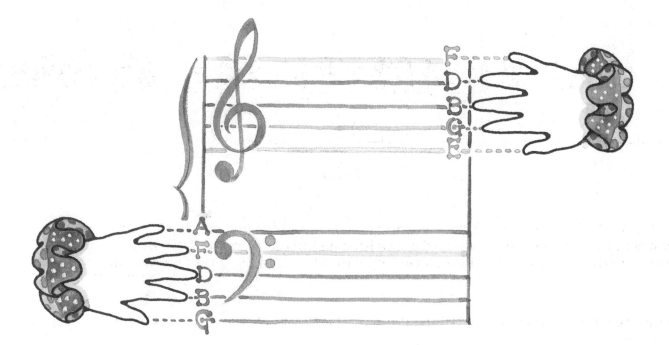

Bass Clef Line Notes

10. Write the letter names of the following bass clef line notes. Play them in the correct place on the keyboard.

1. _____ 2. _____ 3. _____ 4. _____ 5. _____ 6. _____

7. _____ 8. _____ 9. _____ 10. _____ 11. _____ 12. _____

11. Write or say the note value name for the above notes.

1. _*quarter*_ 5. _____ 9. _____

2. _____ 6. _____ 10. _____

3. _____ 7. _____ 11. _____

4. _____ 8. _____ 12. _____

Treble Clef Line Notes

12. Write the letter names of the following treble clef line notes. Play them in the correct place on the keyboard.

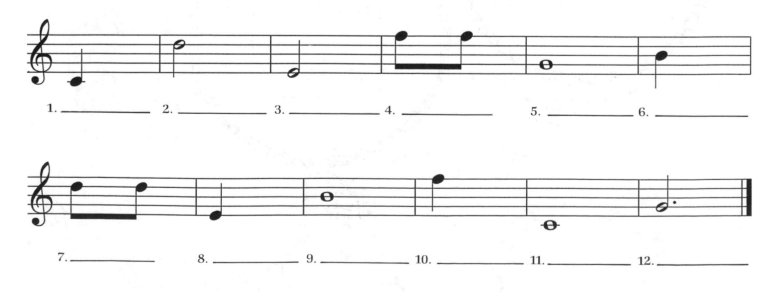

1. _____ 2. _____ 3. _____ 4. _____ 5. _____ 6. _____

7. _____ 8. _____ 9. _____ 10. _____ 11. _____ 12. _____

13. Say the note value name for each of the above treble clef notes.

14. Write the letter names of the notes in each balloon. Write the note value name.

1. _E quarter_

2. ____ _____

3. ____ _____

4. ____ _____

5. ____ _____

6. ____ _____

7. ____ _____

8. ____ _____

9. ____ _____

10. ____ _____

11. ____ _____

12. ____ _____

Drawing Line Notes

15. Draw the following line notes in the bass clef. Play them in the correct place on the keyboard.

16. Listen and draw the note your teacher plays after the given note. (Skip, step, repeat? Up, down?) Write the letter names of the notes you draw.

1. _____ 2. _____ 3. _____ 4. _____ 5. _____

17. Write the number which matches:

1. Skip up _____

2. Step down _____

3. Repeated notes _____

4. Skip down _____

5. Step up _____

18. Draw the following line notes in the treble clef. Play them in the correct place on the keyboard.

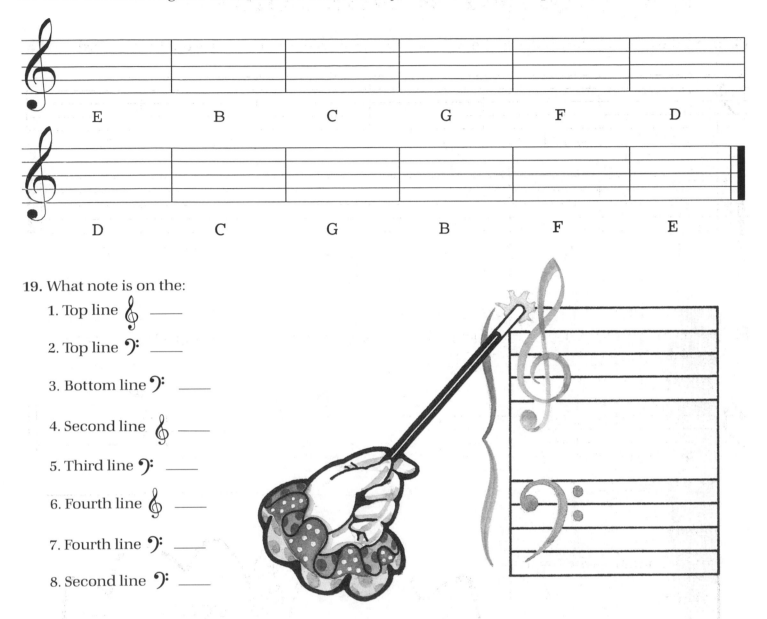

E B C G F D

D C G B F E

19. What note is on the:

1. Top line 𝄞 ———

2. Top line 𝄢 ———

3. Bottom line 𝄢 ———

4. Second line 𝄞 ———

5. Third line 𝄢 ———

6. Fourth line 𝄞 ———

7. Fourth line 𝄢 ———

8. Second line 𝄢 ———

20. Listen and draw the note your teacher plays after the given note. Write the letter names of the notes.

1. ___ ___ 2. ___ ___ 3. ___ ___ 4. ___ ___ 5. ___ ___

6. ___ ___ 7. ___ ___ 8. ___ ___ 9. ___ ___ 10. ___ ___

Space Notes on the Staff

F is in the space below the bass clef.
From a space to a space is a skip.
A skip up from F is A etc.

21. Draw the letter names of the notes in the spaces. Play these notes in the correct place on the keyboard.

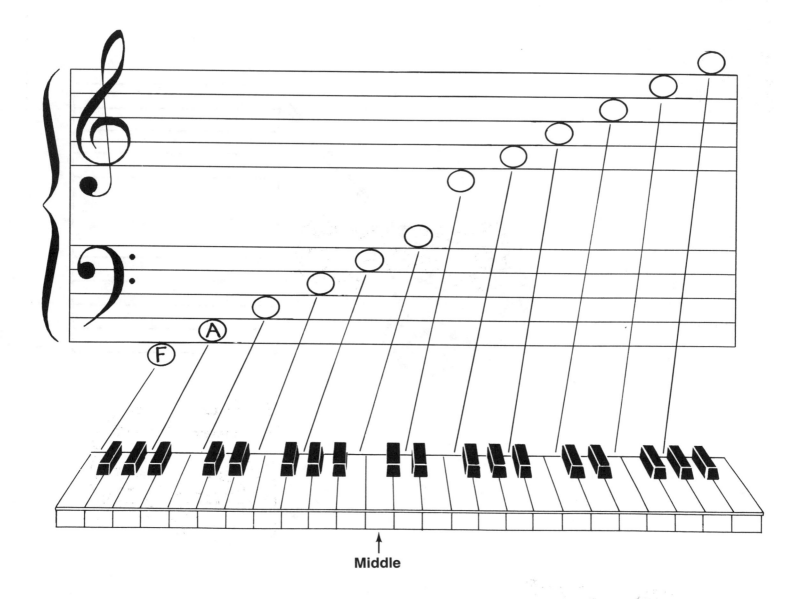

Middle

The notes in the bass staff are found on the lower part of the keyboard.
The notes in the treble staff are found on the upper part of the keyboard.

Practice naming and playing the space notes on the *Bastien Music Flashcards* until you can recognize them easily.

22. Write the letter names of the space notes 4 times a day. Say the letters aloud as you write them. Memorize these letters. Continue, on blank music paper, to write and say the space notes 4 times every day.

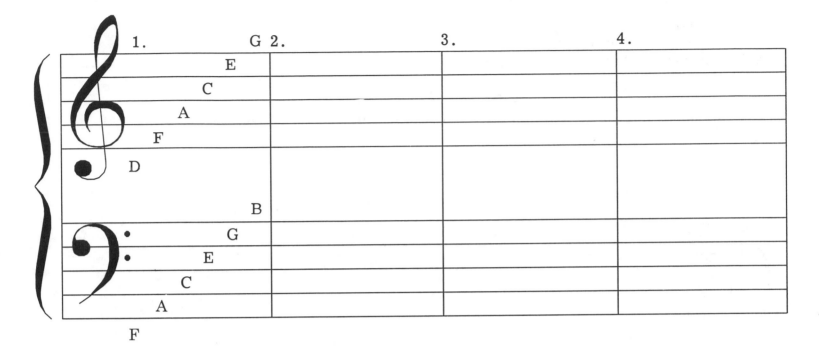

23. Turn your hands sideways (LH   RH). Let the spaces between your fingers represent the spaces of the staff. Point to each space and say its name. You can do this anytime, for example, while riding in the car.

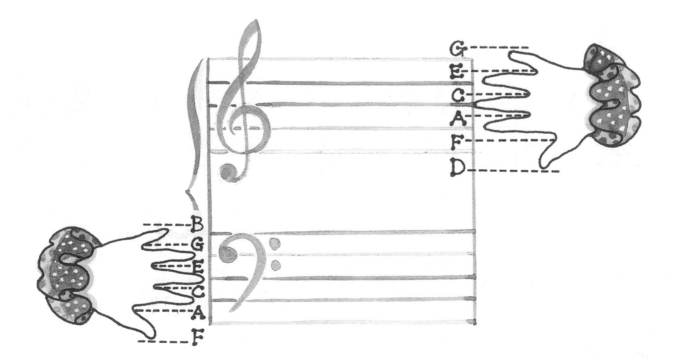

Bass Clef Space Notes

24. Write the letter names of the following bass clef space notes. Play them in the correct place on the keyboard.

1. __C__ 2. ___ 3. ___ 4. ___ 5. ___ 6. ___

7. ___ 8. ___ 9. ___ 10. ___ 11. ___ 12. ___

25. Write or say the note value names for the above notes.

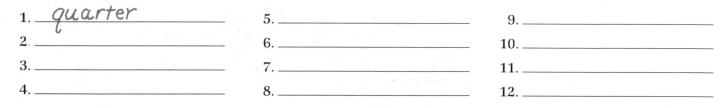

1. _quarter_
2. _____
3. _____
4. _____

5. _____
6. _____
7. _____
8. _____

9. _____
10. _____
11. _____
12. _____

Treble Clef Space Notes

26. Write the letter names of the following treble clef space notes. Play them in the correct place on the keyboard.

1. ___ 2. ___ 3. ___ 4. ___ 5. ___ 6. ___

7. ___ 8. ___ 9. ___ 10. ___ 11. ___ 12. ___

27. Write the letter names of the notes. Write the note value name.

1. <u>F half note</u>   5. ___ _____   9. ___ _____

2. ___ _____   6. ___ _____   10. ___ _____

3. ___ _____   7. ___ _____   11. ___ _____

4. ___ _____   8. ___ _____   12. ___ _____

Drawing Space Notes

28. Draw the following space notes in the bass clef. Play them in the correct place on the keyboard.

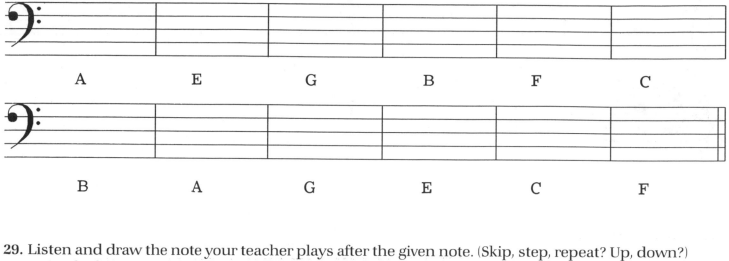

A   E   G   B   F   C

B   A   G   E   C   F

29. Listen and draw the note your teacher plays after the given note. (Skip, step, repeat? Up, down?) Write the letter names of the notes you draw.

1._____ 2._____ 3._____ 4._____ 5._____

30. Write the number which matches the correct notes.

1. B-G _____

2. F-D _____

3. C-E _____

4. G-E _____

5. C-E _____

31. Draw the following space notes in the treble clef. Play them in the correct place on the keyboard.

C   G   E   F   D   A

G   F   C   E   A   D

32. What note is in the:

1. Third space 𝄞 ____

2. Space below 𝄢 ____

3. Second space 𝄞 ____

4. First space 𝄢 ____

5. Space above 𝄞 ____

6. Space above 𝄢 ____

7. Third space 𝄢 ____

8. Space below 𝄞 ____

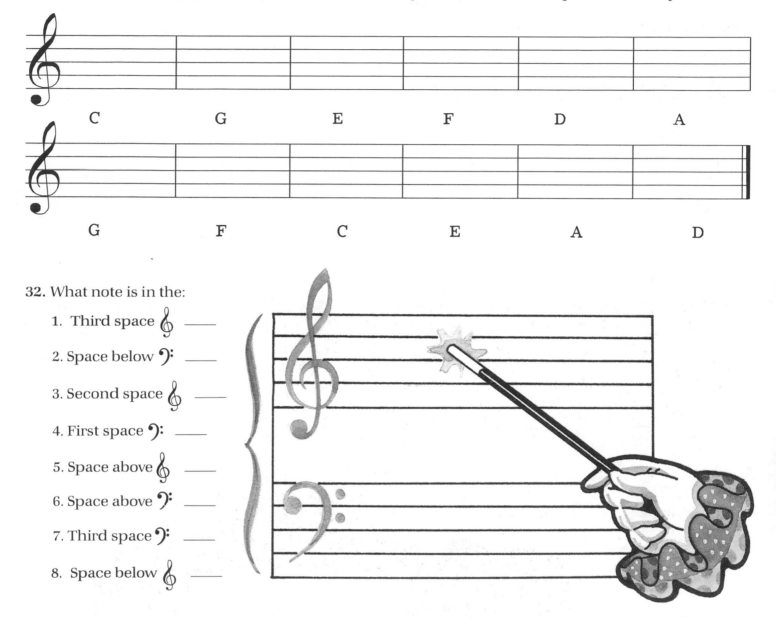

33. Listen and draw the note your teacher plays after the given note. Write the letter names of the notes.

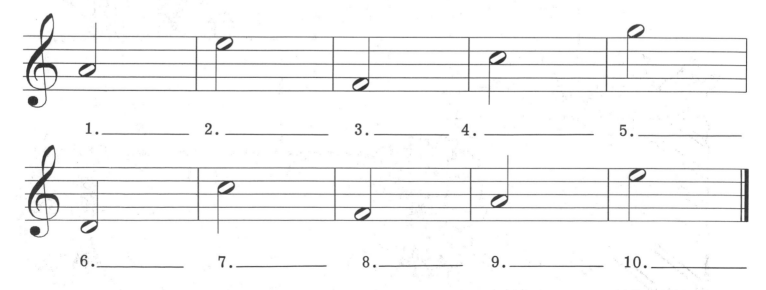

1. _____ 2. _____ 3. _____ 4. _____ 5. _____

6. _____ 7. _____ 8. _____ 9. _____ 10. _____

Naming and Playing Notes

34. Write the letter names of the notes. Observe the clef signs. Play and count the note value names. Do one line a day.

35. Write the letter name of the given note. Listen and draw the next note your teacher plays. Write the letter name of that note. Listen again and color the apples which contain the notes your teacher plays.

Note to teachers: Students should listen for high and low sounds to distinguish which example is being played.

Naming and Playing Notes

36. Write the letter names of the notes. Observe the clef signs. Play and count the note value names. Do one line a day.

Listening

37. Write the letter name of the given note. Listen and draw the next note your teacher plays. Write the letter name of that note. Listen again and point to the bubble that has the notes your teacher plays.

Note to teachers: Play only a skip or step up or down from given notes. Students should listen for high and low sounds to distinguish which example is being played.

Drawing and Playing Notes

38. Draw the following **line** notes. Play and count the note value names.

39. Draw the following **space** notes. Play and count the note value names.

40. Draw the following **line** notes. Play and count the note value names.

41. Draw the following **space** notes. Play and count the note value names.

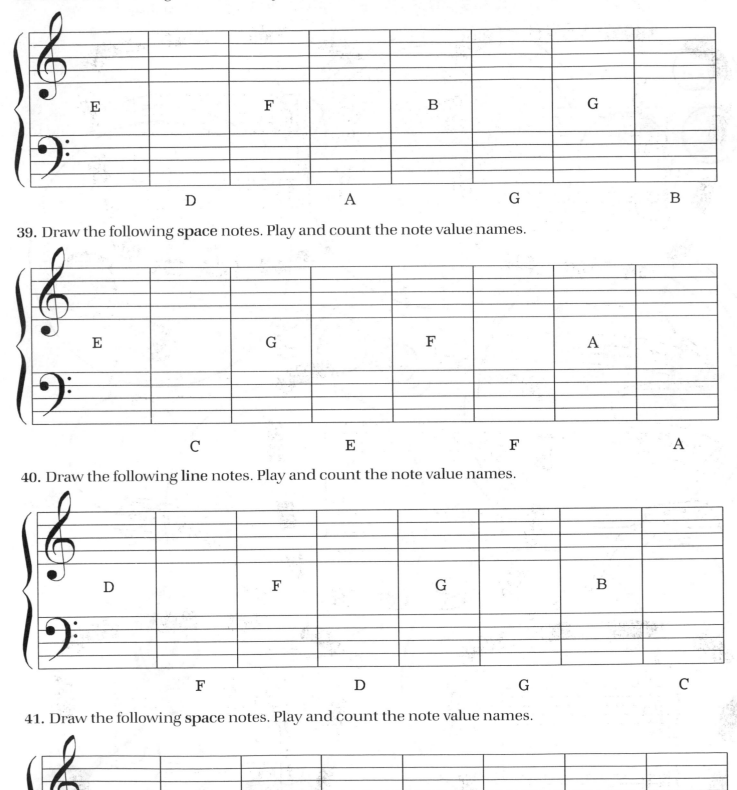

Listening

42. Listen to your teacher play C, E, G. Draw the notes in the correct place on the staff.

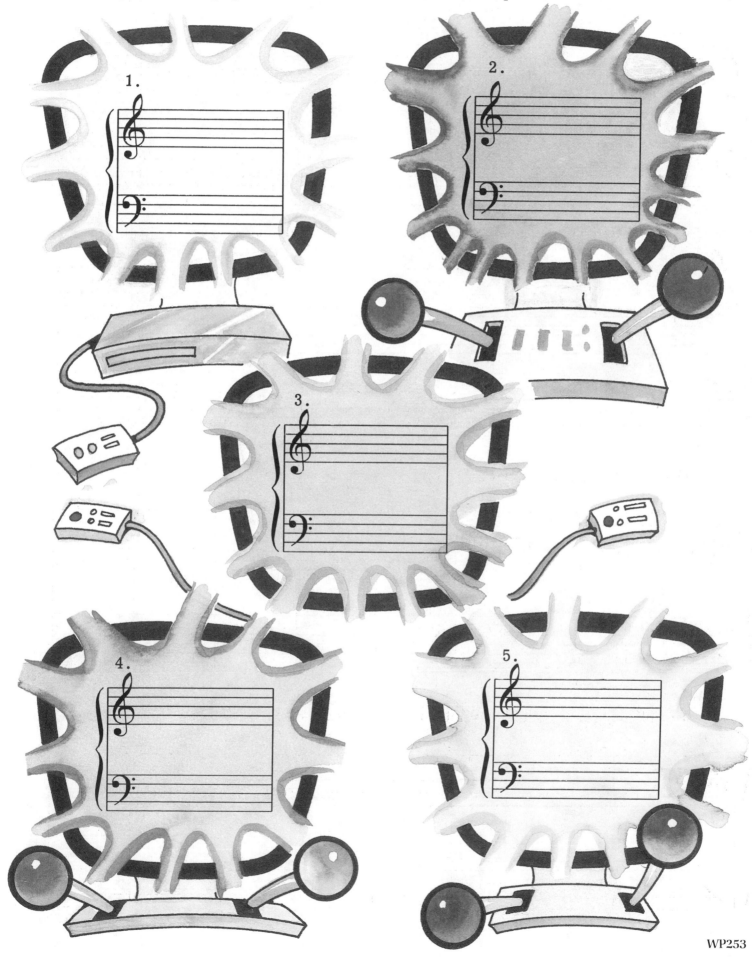

Note Spelling

43. Write the letter names of the notes in order to spell words.

Listening

44. Listen to your teacher play G, A, B. Draw the notes in the correct place on the staff.

Keyboard and Staff Matching

45. Write the notes numbered on the keyboard
in the correct place on the staves.

Listening

46. Listen as your teacher plays the given note, and draw it in the correct place on the staff.

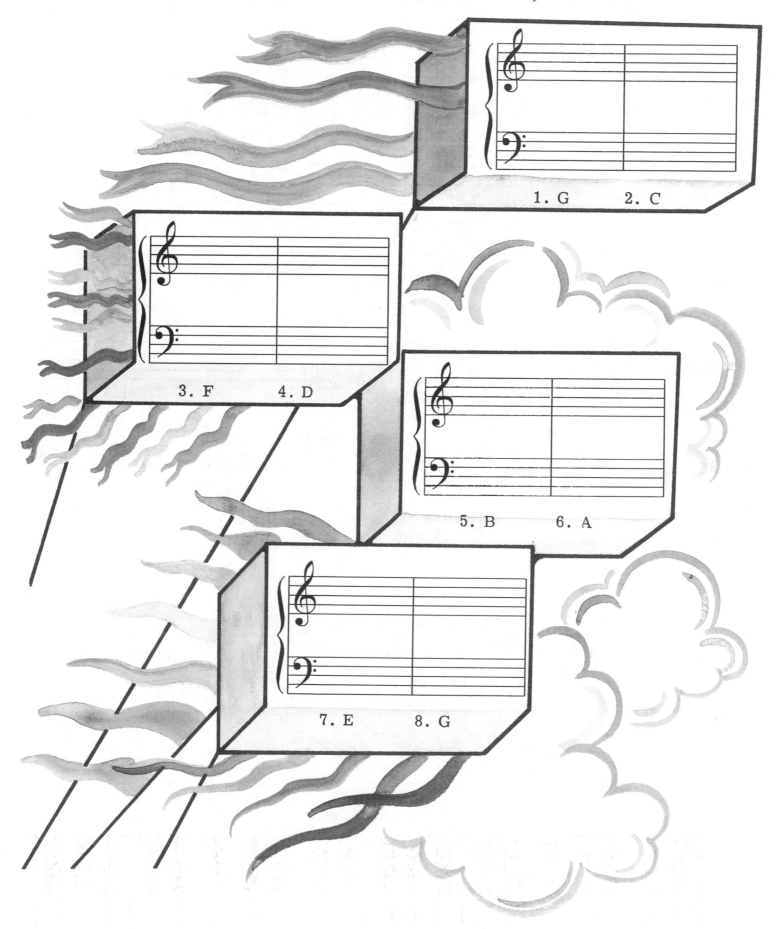

1. G   2. C

3. F   4. D

5. B   6. A

7. E   8. G

One Minute, Please!

47. Every day this week, point to each note and say its letter name. Time yourself with a stopwatch
and try to say all the notes in one minute or less. At the end of the week, time yourself and write
in the letter names of the notes.

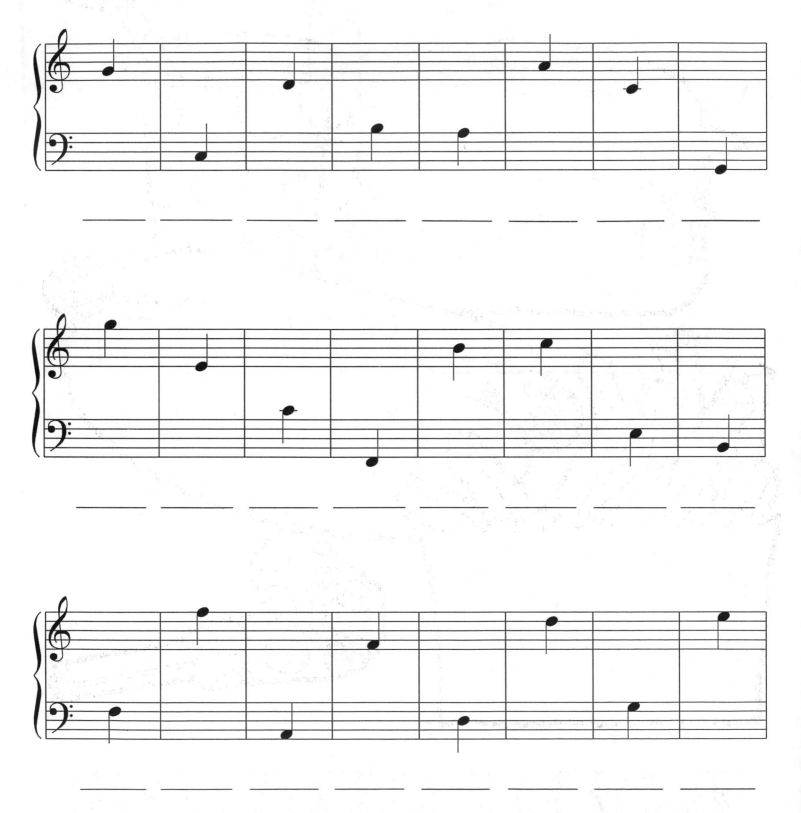

Time: _____

Keyboard and Staff Matching

48. Write the notes numbered on the keyboard in the correct place on the staves.

One Minute Practice

49. Write the letter names of the notes and time yourself. Can you do it in one minute? Play the notes on the piano. How quickly can you do this?

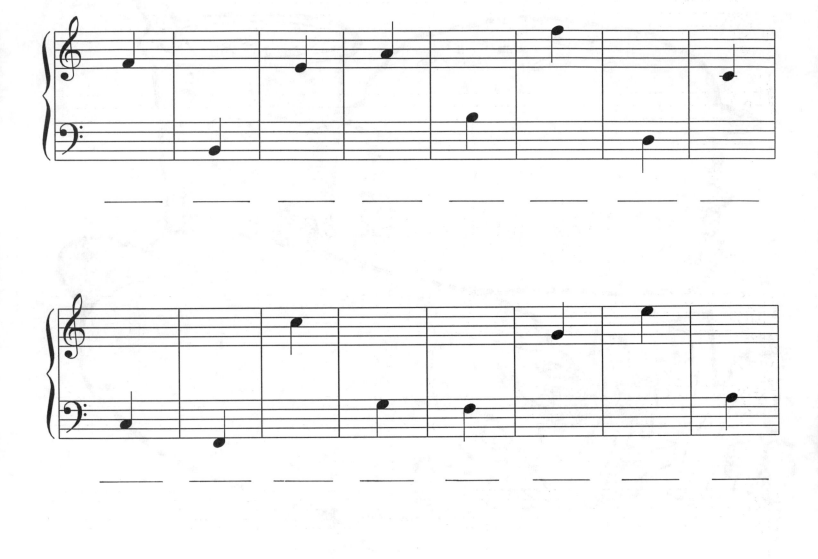

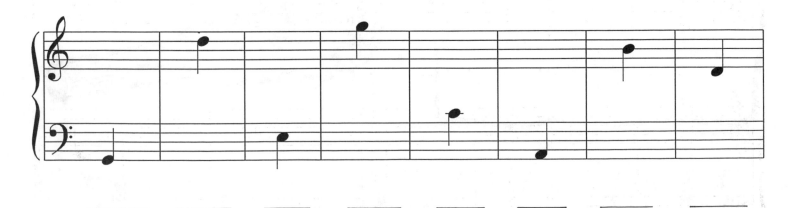

Time: _____

Listening

50. Listen to the note your teacher plays and draw it in the correct place on the staff. Now listen and draw the next note your teacher plays. Write the letter name of the second note.

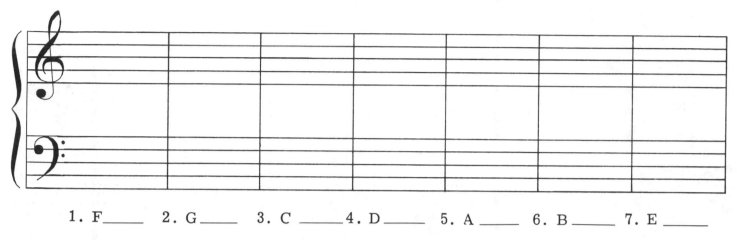

1. F_____   2. G_____   3. C_____   4. D_____   5. A_____   6. B_____   7. E_____

One Minute Practice

51. Write the letter names of the notes and time yourself. Play the notes on the piano and time yourself.

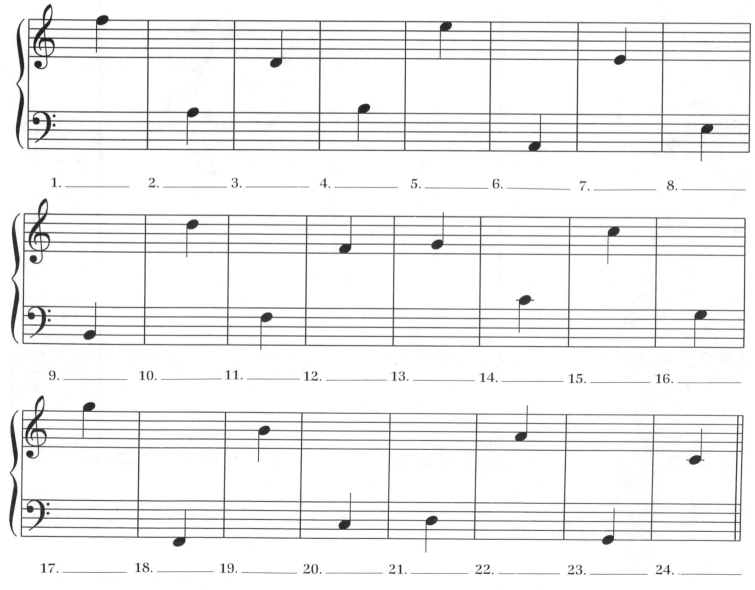

1. _____   2. _____   3. _____   4. _____   5. _____   6. _____   7. _____   8. _____

9. _____   10. _____   11. _____   12. _____   13. _____   14. _____   15. _____   16. _____

17. _____   18. _____   19. _____   20. _____   21. _____   22. _____   23. _____   24. _____

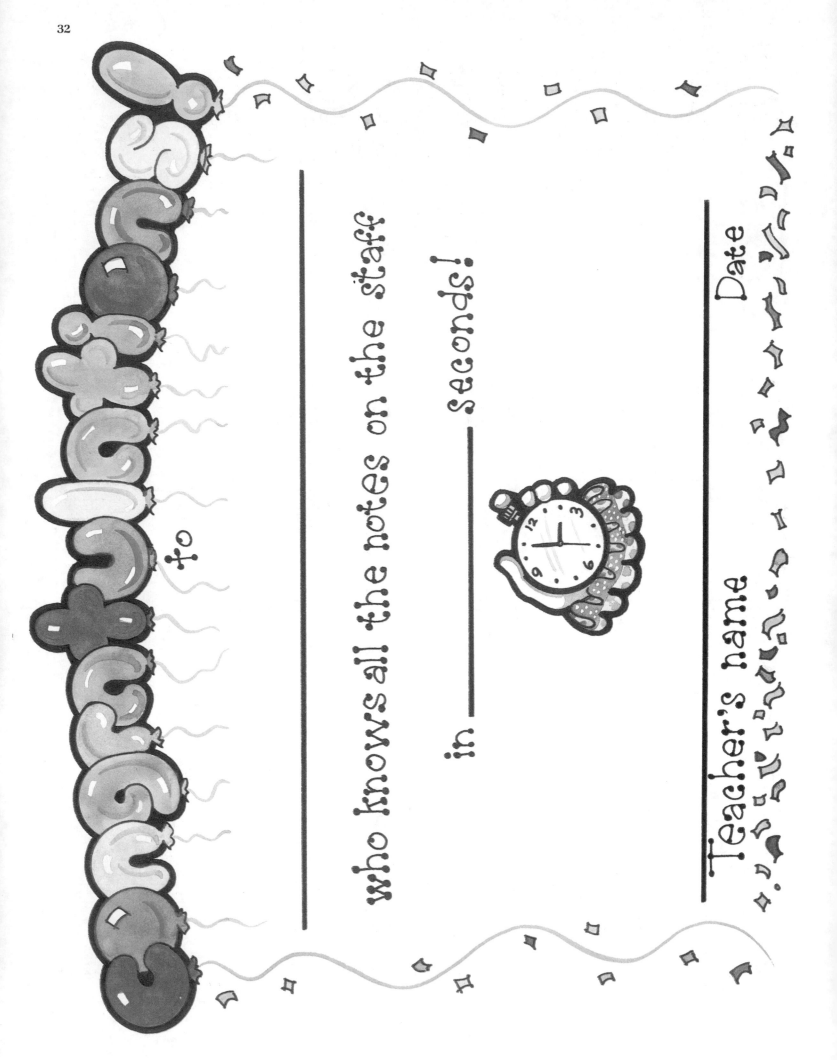

Congratulations!

to _____

who knows all the notes on the staff

in _____ seconds!

_____
Teacher's name

_____
Date